ROSE CREEK PUBLIC LIBRARY
4476 TOWNE LAKE PKWY.
WOODSTOCK, GA 30189

JERRY SLOAN

SCOTTIE PIPPEN

ARTIS GILMORE

MICHAEL JORDAN

HORACE GRANT

RON ARTEST

BOB BOOZER

BILL CARTWRIGHT

DENNIS RODMAN

ELTON BRAND

ORLANDO WOOLRIDGE

CHET WALKER

CREATIVE C EDUCATION
JOHN NICHOLS

Published by Creative Education, 123 South Broad Street, Mankato, MN 56001

Creative Education is an imprint of The Creative Company.

Designed by Rita Marshall

Photos by Allsport, AP/Wide World, Rich Kane, NBA Photos, SportsChrome

Library of Congress Cataloging-in-Publication Data

Nichols, John, 1966-  The history of the Chicago Bulls / by John Nichols.

p. cm. — (Pro basketball today)   ISBN 1-58341-093-7

1. Chicago Bulls (Basketball team)—History—

Juvenile literature. [1. Chicago Bulls (Basketball team)—History.

2. Basketball—History.] I. Title. II. Series.

GV885.52.C45 N53 2001      796.323'64'0977311—dc21      00-047341

First Edition  9 8 7 6 5 4 3 2 1

# CHICAGO, ILLINOIS, WAS

## FOUNDED IN THE 1830S AND

### GREW RAPIDLY TO BECOME THE UNITED STATES' CENTER

for grain and livestock trade. Situated on the western shores of Lake

Michigan, Chicago is known as the "Windy City," since its streets and

buildings are constantly buffeted by strong gusts that howl in off the

lake. To Chicago's citizens, the brisk winds are an everyday reminder

that a person has to be tough to live there.

The people of Chicago are fiercely proud of their city, and it

shows in the way they support their professional sports teams. In 1966,

Chicago was granted a franchise in the National Basketball Association

## BOB BOOZER

(NBA). Given the city's long history as a cattle town, coming up with a team name was easy. The franchise was called the Chicago Bulls, a name that symbolizes strength, size, and a powerful will.

{BULLS COME OUT CHARGING} Most expansion teams have a hard time winning games. But the 1966–67 Chicago Bulls were a pleasant surprise. Head coach Johnny "Red" Kerr put together a solid club that featured

In the Bulls' first season, Guy Rodgers set a team record with 24 assists in one game.

two steady veterans, guard Guy Rodgers and forward Bob Boozer, and a hard-nosed second-year guard by the name of Jerry Sloan.

The 6-foot-5 and 195-pound Sloan was acquired by the Bulls in the expansion draft from the Baltimore Bullets. A little-used reserve as a rookie in Baltimore, Sloan took advantage of the opportunity to start in Chicago. "In his first year with us, he led the league in floor burns and fights in practice," joked Coach Kerr.

# SCOTTIE PIPPEN

Guard Jerry Sloan won Chicago fans over with his scrappy style of play.

JERRY SLOAN

Sloan's warrior-like attitude sparked Chicago to 33 wins in its first year—an NBA record for an expansion team—and the upstart Bulls made the playoffs. After yet another playoff berth in 1968, Kerr left the Bulls and was replaced by an obscure college coach named Dick Motta, who quickly gained a reputation as a top strategist and motivator.

Motta's strength was in devising defensive schemes that took advantage of his team's bruising style. By 1972, he had built a starting lineup that included the always combative Sloan, scrappy point guard Norm Van Lier, and hulking 7-foot and 265-pound center Tom Boerwinkle. The offensive punch came from smooth forwards Chet Walker and Bob Love. "Playing the Bulls is like running through a barbed wire fence," muttered Los Angeles Lakers guard Gail Goodrich. "You may win the game, but they're gonna put lumps on you."

In one **1969–70** game, big center Tom Boerwinkle racked up an amazing 37 rebounds.

**9**

# TOM BOERWINKLE

Forwards Bob Love (#10) and Cliff Ray (#14) led the Bulls in the early **'70s**.

BOB LOVE

During Motta's eight-year tenure, the Bulls won 50 or more games four times and made the playoffs six times. Unfortunately, his teams

were never quite good enough to make it to the top. By 1976, the feisty Bulls had grown old. Walker retired, and a chronic knee injury forced the team's ultimate warrior, Jerry Sloan, to retire after 11 seasons.

{CHICAGO RIDES THE "A-TRAIN"} During the late 1970s and early '80s, the Bulls faded in the standings. The Chicago franchise was left in disarray as it hired and fired seven different coaches in as many seasons. Although they saw few victories, Bulls fans did enjoy some great individual performances.

Prior to the 1976–77 season, Chicago acquired powerful 7-foot-2 and 250-pound center Artis Gilmore. Known as the "A-Train" because of his enormous size and strength, Gilmore had spent five seasons in

CHET WALKER

the rival American Basketball Association (ABA). After the ABA merged

with the NBA, a dispersal draft was held for ABA players who no longer

had a team. Gilmore was the prize of the draft, and the Bulls selected

him with the first overall pick.

Gilmore's arrival stirred hopes that the Bulls could become a

contender again. In his first season, Gilmore averaged 18 points,

13 rebounds, and almost 3 blocked shots a game. Winning 20 of their final 24 games, the Bulls went 44–38 and returned to the playoffs in 1977. Although Gilmore and the Bulls were quickly eliminated by the Portland Trail Blazers in the postseason, the A-Train brought new hope to Chicago fans.

Gilmore continued to shine over the next few seasons, averaging more than 20 points and 12 rebounds a game, but the team's fortunes shifted. In 1982, the Bulls dipped to last place in their division and missed the playoffs. After the season, the organization decided to rebuild with younger players such as high-scoring guard Reggie Theus and explosive forward Orlando Woolridge.

That year, the 33-year-old Gilmore was traded to the San Antonio Spurs. "It's a shame we couldn't put a better team around Artis," noted teammate Norm Van Lier. "He did everything he could, but when we

In **1980–81**, All-Star guard Reggie Theus led Chicago with close to 19 points a game.

**ARTIS GILMORE**

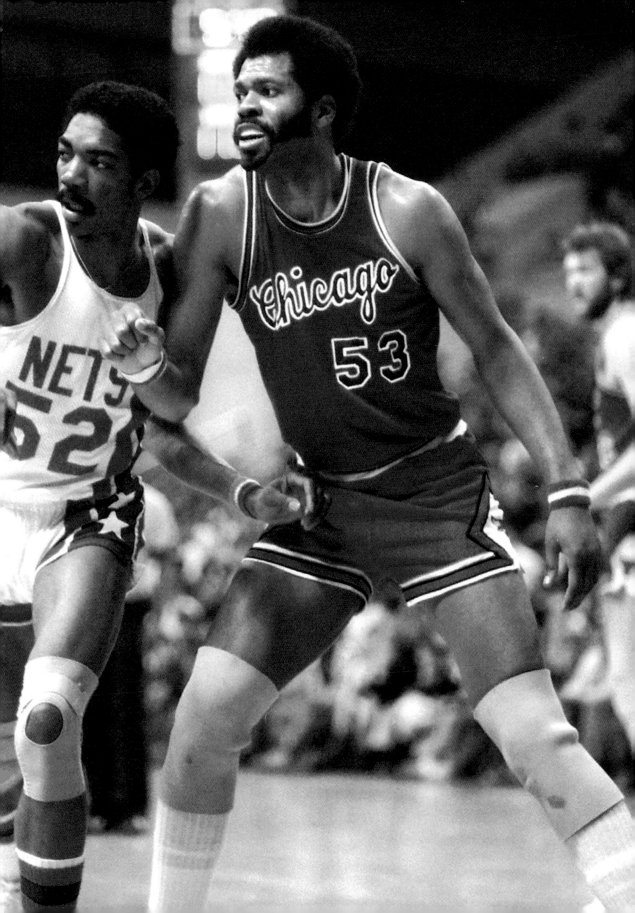

lost, he always got the blame." Despite his best efforts, the A-Train did

not prove to be the savior Chicago fans hoped he would be. But that

long-awaited savior would soon arrive.

{WINDY CITY WELCOMES "AIR JORDAN"} In 1984, the

Bulls held the third overall pick in the NBA Draft. Coming off a 27–55

season, the Bulls needed help at every position. But when it came time to choose, the Bulls took a 6-foot-6 and 200-pound guard by the name

of Michael Jordan.

Jordan, a two-time college All-American at the

University of North Carolina, had exceptional talent, but

no one could have anticipated the shockwave he would

send through the NBA. With unstoppable moves, explo-

sive quickness, and unrivaled leaping ability, Jordan

Like Artis Gilmore, forward Charles Oakley was a low-post tower of strength in the **'80s**.

soared to dizzying heights, averaging 28 points and nearly 6 assists a

game as a rookie. His in-flight acrobatics quickly earned him the nick-

name "Air Jordan." "I've never seen a rookie who can take over a game

the way that he can," said Los Angeles Lakers star Magic Johnson.

Over the next few seasons, Jordan continued to sparkle, but

Chicago remained an average team. The Bulls front office knew that

Jordan needed some help. So, in the 1987 NBA Draft, the team chose

# CHARLES OAKLEY

In 12 superb seasons, Michael Jordan earned six NBA titles and legendary status.

athletic power forward Horace Grant and traded with Seattle for the draft rights to multitalented forward Scottie Pippen.

With Grant, Pippen, and Jordan, the Bulls became a powerhouse in the Eastern Conference. However, Chicago's quest for an NBA championship in the late '80s was consistently thwarted by one team—the rough-and-tumble Detroit Pistons. From 1988 to 1990, the Pistons,

led by star point guard Isiah Thomas, knocked the young Bulls out of the playoffs every year.

The veteran Pistons slowed the Bulls by physically pounding the high-flying Pippen and Jordan. With a bigger lineup, the Pistons tried to intimidate the Bulls, and it worked. "They got in our head with the physical stuff," admitted Pippen. "But in doing it, the Pistons taught us the toughness we needed."

# PHIL JACKSON

{THE BULLS BREAK OUT} At the start of the 1990–91 season, the

Bulls were confident that their time had come. Head coach Phil Jackson,

who arrived in Chicago a year earlier, had convinced the Bulls that

although Jordan was their star, it would take a team effort to win a title.

Chicago rolled through the regular season with a 61–21 record. In

the playoffs, the Bulls charged all the way to the Eastern Conference

Finals. Laying in wait was their old nemesis, the Detroit Pistons. This

time the Bulls would not be intimidated. Jordan, Pippen, and Grant

dominated their old foes, eliminating the Pistons in four

straight games.

In the Finals, Chicago faced another proud, veteran

team in the Los Angeles Lakers. Lakers guard Magic

Johnson pulled out a victory in game one for Los Angeles,

but after that, it was all Chicago as the Bulls swept the next four games.

After a 25-year wait, Chicago finally had its first NBA championship.

"It's been a long, hard road," said guard John Paxson. "We knew if we all

pulled together, we could get it done."

The wait would not be so long for the second title. The next sea-

son, the Bulls trampled the opposition on their way to a 67–15 record.

They then topped New York and Cleveland to earn a trip to the NBA

# CRAIG HODGES

Horace Grant was the Bulls' top rebounder in six of his seven seasons in Chicago.

HORACE GRANT

Finals against the Portland Trail Blazers. Led by their now battle-hard-

ened starting five of Jordan, Pippen, Grant, point guard B.J. Armstrong,

and center Bill Cartwright, the Bulls hammered out a

four-games-to-two victory over Portland.

The Bulls captured a third consecutive champi-

onship in 1993, beating the Phoenix Suns in six games.

Then, things changed dramatically for the team. Jordan,

feeling he had nothing more to prove, decided to retire. At age 30, the

NBA's best player walked away to pursue a career in professional base-

ball. Although the Bulls added talented European swingman Toni Kukoc

in 1994, the Bulls' drive for a fourth straight title was snuffed out in the

playoffs by the New York Knicks.

{SUPERMAN'S RETURN} Going into the 1994–95 season, the

Bulls were forced to make some adjustments. The team lost veteran cen-

> Swingman Toni Kukoc picked up much of the scoring slack after Jordan's retirement in **1993**.

25

# TONI KUKOC

ter Bill Cartwright to retirement, and Horace Grant left town as a free

agent. But the team did manage to sign guard Ron Harper, a former All-

Star. The new-look Bulls struggled to stay above .500, but in March

1995, fortune smiled on the team. After a year and a half away from the

game, Jordan decided to return.

The city of Chicago was breathless with anticipation. Many fans thought that Jordan would magically lift the Bulls to another championship. The Bulls did improve with the addition of Jordan, but his game was not quite the same. Although he still scored almost 27 points per game, he lacked the explosiveness that had been his trademark for so long. Jordan didn't even look the same. He decided to wear jersey number 45, since his usual number 23 had already been retired by the team.

With almost 15 boards a game, Dennis Rodman led the NBA in rebounding in **1995–96**.

In the playoffs, Jordan and the Bulls fell to the Orlando Magic. Afterward, Orlando guard Nick Anderson told reporters that the new Jordan wasn't equal to the old. "That number 45, he isn't Superman," Anderson said. "Number 23 was, but this guy isn't."

The loss to the Magic and the sting of such criticism inspired Jordan, who went back to his old jersey number and spent the off-season refining his game. The Bulls then added eccentric power forward

# DENNIS RODMAN

Dennis Rodman to the lineup. "Dennis looks weird and he does a lot of crazy things, but he's also the best rebounder in basketball," noted Pippen. "We need him to get where we want to go."

With Jordan back to his dominant ways and Rodman supplying the muscle, the Bulls ran roughshod over the league in 1995–96. Chicago's 72–10 regular-season mark set a new NBA record for most wins in a season. In the playoffs, the Bulls charged to their fourth championship in six years. "This means a lot to me," said an emotional Jordan. "People doubted us. We proved them wrong."

Over the next two seasons, no one doubted the Bulls, as the quintet of Jordan, Pippen, Rodman, Harper, and Kukoc, along with center Luc Longley and key reserve guard Steve Kerr, stampeded to two more championships. In 1997, a flu-stricken Jordan defied his illness and pow-

Luc Longley, a native of Australia, manned the middle for Chicago in the mid-**1990s**.

LUC LONGLEY

ered the Bulls to a Finals triumph over the Utah Jazz. The next year, Jordan poured in 45 points—including the game-winning basket—in game six to top the Jazz for the title yet again.

{A NEW GENERATION OF BULLS} After a 12-year career in which he won five NBA Most Valuable Player awards and led the league in scoring 10 times, Michael Jordan retired for good in 1998. Shortly afterwards, coach Phil Jackson left the team, Scottie Pippen was traded away, and Dennis Rodman left as a free agent. One of the greatest dynasties in NBA history was over.

Looking to rebuild, the team hired former college coach Tim Floyd as its new head man. The Bulls struggled in Floyd's first two seasons as young players such as center Elton Brand, forward Ron Artest, and guard Corey Benjamin gained valuable experience. Fans hoped that

Veteran guard Hersey Hawkins led the young Bulls in three-point shooting in **1999–00**.

# HERSEY HAWKINS

Tough center
Elton Brand
succeeded
Michael Jordan
as the Bulls'
on-court
leader.

ELTON BRAND

Chicago
continued to
rebuild in
**2000–01** with
the addition of
guard Ron
Mercer.

RON MERCER

these players, along with potential stars such as forward Marcus Fizer

and speedy point guard Khalid El-Amin, would carry the team back

among the league's elite.

Quick yet powerful forward Ron Artest showed the potential to be a premier defender.

For more than 35 years, the Chicago Bulls have played

a prominent role in the story of the NBA. Through the

team's many highs and lows, there has always been one

constant in Chicago—toughness. Backed by a city known

32 for its strong will, the time may soon come when the Bulls charge back

into contention.

# RON ARTEST